Horst Hamann

New York
vertical

teNeues

A Production by EDITION**PANORAMA** Germany

New York

vertical

Contents

Preface   7
Volker Skierka

Verticals   15

Information
Map   151
Vertical Information   152

New York,
the vertical challenge   159
Horst Hamann

Biography   162

Volker Skierka, born in 1952, was managing editor of the Hamburg-based culture and travel magazine Merian from 1992 to 1997. Before that, he worked for 13 years as correspondent for the Süddeutsche Zeitung in Berlin, northern Europe as well as in Latin America based in Santiago de Chile. He began his journalistic career for the Nürnberger Nachrichten, and later worked as a correspondent for the British news agency Reuters. He is a winner of the Egon-Erwin-Kisch-Reportage-Award and author of several books.

New York Vertical

Volker Skierka

Arriving is the best part of traveling. For me, no arrival was more beautiful or more exalting than the one I had on the Queen Elizabeth II to New York. After a five-day Atlantic crossing, as the New York skyline moved closer in the early morning sunlight, the skyscrapers released themselves from the mist, towering denser and higher, as the oceanliner slowly cruised by the proud Statue of Liberty, it was as though the uplifting symphony From the New World was playing for us new arrivals who stood on deck, amazed and in excited anticipation, shivering in the light morning wind. Antonín Dvořák composed the piece at the end of the 19th century during his three years as director of the National Conservatory in New York. This musical work dramatically packaged the sensations of the millions who for centuries arrived by water, full of hope and expectation of adventure in New York and America. Very few of them, however, traveled on luxury steamers. Most of the fortune seekers arrived in the New World crammed en masse on immigrant ships. Their first stop was Ellis Island in the shadows of the 150-foot-high, copper-green, torch-bearing Miss Liberty, a gift from the French people to the Americans in 1886. They had to survive the immigrant processing before they were allowed to ferry across to Manhattan. With his 1925 novel Manhattan Transfer, the American writer John Dos Passos created a literary monument to them. From one generation to the next, these people, together with New York, created an immortal monument. They made this city quite simply the "City of Cities". For all time. The city rests on firm pillars, just as its predecessors did. "There were Babylon and Nineveh; they were built of brick. Athens was gold marble columns. In Constantinople the minarets flame already shooting up. The 308-foot Flatiron Building in the sharp angle at Fifth Avenue and Broadway was built in 1902; the Metropolitan Life Tower, a looming, over-sized 692-foot copy of the Campanile in Venice, rose up from Madison Square in 1909; in 1913 the Woolworth Building at 783 feet took its place on Broadway and in the record books where it reigned as the highest building in the world until 1930.

With the completion of the 1036-foot, art deco Chrysler Building, a stormy era in skyscraper construction began. The building style released itself from its European model at the same time corporations began erecting their own skyscrapers as a mark of their economic potency. For John Jacob Raskob, vice president of General Motors, this was the motivation to go higher and outdo his competition at Chrysler. The story goes that he took hold of a fat pencil, stood it upright on his desk and asked his architect, "Bill, how high can you build without its falling down?" The result was the Empire State Building, put up in a record time of 13 months and dedicated in May 1931. At just about 1248 feet, it remained the highest building in the world until the completion of the 1375-foot World Trade Center in 1973. In the 1930s and 1940s, Rockefeller Center was created as "the democratic American answer to the fascist and communist monumental architecture". Consisting of 19 buildings, green spaces, fountains and sculptures, it is a city within a city where 65,000 people work and 175,000 visitors stream in and out every day.

The aesthetics that emerged as the backdrop to the struggle for survival and pursuit of profit is unique in this world. And unsurpassed. There are other well-known vertical skyscrapers, soarers, residential highrises and office towers, that are even higher. Or more radical. Or more futuristic. For some time now New York has not been home to the highest building in the world. Still to this day, no other city has been able to match New York's architectural mix of Colonial and Federal, Greek and Roman Revival, neo-Classic and neo-Gothic, Beaux-Arts, Modern Streamline, Art Deco and Postmodern. Whatever the name — Hong Kong or Shanghai, Tokyo or Singapore, Chicago, São Paulo, Moscow or Frankfurt — all are just imitations. All these cities may possess a dynamic, exotic or cool charm and may be open for a serious flirtation or a casual affair. But none of them has that which makes up New York's uniqueness and its power of attraction — its legends and its myths, its copious stories that are repeated every day in the major and minor reports of success and failure. New York invokes yearning despite the horror stories about criminal activity and isolation. Where else is the mix of reality and fiction so great that it all can be true? New York produces the stuff of dreams — of making money, of literature art and music, and above all, movies and television. Why shouldn't Fritz Lang's Metropolis still be a piece of reality somewhere in the underground? Or that unforgettable Breakfast at Tiffany's? Or Woody Allen's neurotic character in Annie Hall in a city filled with neurotics? A mutant gorilla like King Kong hanging onto the Empire State Building seems just as plausible as a flaming inferno in a skyscraper. And didn't Crocodile Dundee from the Australian bush also land in New York with which the film became a hit, proving once again the truth of the motto — A few New York scenes are always good for the box office.

The simple secret of the city is that it is in and of itself enough and every day its insurpassable production tests the limits of credibility. The potential from which the city draws its attractiveness, its energy, fantasy and creativity are the people, this ethnic mixture on the streets and behind the facades of the cement cathedrals, their exotic and banal aromas, their noises. It is by day and by night the special play of light and shadows between the high-rises. And it is the capacity for whirling regeneration. Like a vamp, the city takes from each one what she needs for her glittering appearance. There is hardly anyone who does not succumb to the fascination of this city; many become hooked.

Horst Hamann, for example. "The city has moved me since my first visit, since I first set eyes on it." Since that first visit, he has lived in New York, specifically in lower Manhattan, for many years. From his studio he can look out at the skyline. He has come to know the city as few others do. He has run all over the city — with the New York gait. This style of walking can be found only here: the fast, regular strides combined with a distinctive bodily elegance when moving out of the way, passing and forging ahead, all executed with modulated breathing. Manhattan is, unlike many other American metropolises, a city for pedestrians, but not for strollers. They disturb the pace. Edward T. Koch, former Mayor of the city of New York puts it this way: "Being a New Yorker means that you have lived here for at least six months. If after that time you find that you walk faster, talk faster, and think faster, you are a New Yorker: It's a state of mind."

At some point this characteristic, the never-ending striving for the top, attracted Hamann's attention. He saw that the architecture with its tradition, its modernness and its breaches reflected the city dwellers and their situation. But it is not only in the grand architecture towering to infinity, but also in the small things, in the details, whether they are on the street or in backyards. Even the most wretched corner is a view of something big, perhaps a landmark waiting to be released that from a distance, like a finger raised in the haze, is a reminder that says "never give up".

And so the idea ripened in the photographer. He would convert his observations artistically, tip his Linhof-Panorama camera 90 degrees and photograph this "vertical city" in its "verticality". No one before him had done that. Hamann, along with the publisher Bernhard Wipfler, developed the idea for this black and white-photography book New York Vertical in 1991 for the Edition Quadrat in Mannheim. Five years of work on the book followed, simultaneous with photo assignments for countless magazines and businesses.

Another photographer also had become fascinated by the idea of capturing the most-photographed city in the world in a undreamed-of way. In 1980 Reinhart Wolf published a book of color photos taken from the tops of New York's most eminent high-rises. He showed the crowns and battlements, the spires and gables of the palaces and cathedrals of capitalism in all their glory and majestic splendor. He shot the buildings from the chief executive suites opposite them and not from the street so that one could see their claim to power in all their details.

Hamann, however, consistently chose the vertical panorama perspective, mostly shooting upwards. When he photographed from a high point, such as the Manhattan Bridge or the Statue of Liberty's crown, he exploited the potential of the vertical format and connected what was happening far below to the whole picture. The fact that Horst Hamann does not consider himself a documentary photographer of architecture is apparent with a quick look at the photos.

The viewer is confronted with surprising perspectives that generate equal amounts of harmony and tension. Hamann confesses that it took one year to learn to use his vertical view and to master the large-format panorama so that he could avoid overloading and meaningless emptiness in the photographs. In the following four years he learned how to handle the unusual 3:1 format as no other. Distorting lines were intentionally put in to emphasize the vertical infinity and to create, in the truest sense of the word, high tension. With his other photography work Hamann has repeatedly broken with convention. His photographs contain only the bare essentials and carry his stark, graphic trademark.

The selection of "verticals" in this book give some idea of how much visual competence, energy and endurance were necessary to find locations and perspectives, the right floor, spot, angle, and position of the sun. The final difficulty was often finding someone who would grant Hamann the access to take his photographs. If that didn't work, Hamann called on a bit of cheek and some luck to get past them, as was the case with the Chrysler Building. When friends of his on a film crew received special permission to shoot at the top of his favorite skyscraper, Hamann sneaked in with them, got off the elevator on the 61st floor and climbed through an office window to shoot what he'd wanted for a long time: the chrome eagle. Due to the light condition and the danger of being discovered, he had just a few minutes to choose his shot. While the traffic droned on 900 feet below, he took his picture: hand-held.

verticals

No matter how you look at New York City – vertically, horizontally, upside down, sideways **– one thing remains clear.** New York City is the Capital of the World.

Rudolph W. Giuliani, former Mayor of the City of New York

No one should come to New York to live unless he is willing to be lucky.

E.B. White, editor and writer

**Who the hell
looks up,**
in this town?
Who has time?

David Zickerman, New Yorker

Most of the people living in New York have come here from the farm to try to make enough money **to go back to the farm.**

Don Marquis, American poet

The present in New York is so powerful **that** the past is lost.

John Jay Chapman, American writer

There is no hope for New Yorkers,
for they glory in their skyscraping sins;
but in Brooklyn
there is the wisdom of the lowly.

Christopher Morley, American novelist

In the last 12 months,
many of my friends
have advised me
to leave New York.

Noritoshi Hirakawa, artist

When it's three o'clock **in New York,** it's still 1938 **in London.**

Bette Midler, singer and actress

**I found New York the way I expected it to be;
a kind of immense vertical mess set
upon a square horizontal order.**

Nicolas Nabokov, Russian composer

One belongs to New York instantly, one belongs to it as much in five minutes as in five years.

Thomas Wolfe, American writer

New York is obviously
built to take off.

Serafine Klarwein, a. m. artist

The only real **advantage of New York is that all its inhabitants ascend to heaven right after their deaths, having served their** full term in hell **right on Manhattan Island.**

Barnard College Bulletin

New York is like a "roach motel"
once you check in, **you never check out!**

Marcus Nispel, director

New York is a great city to live in **if you can afford** to get out of **it.**

William Rossa Cole, American writer

There is something in the New York air that makes sleep useless.

Simone de Beauvoir, French novelist

And we will probably be judged **not by the monuments** we build **but by those** we have destroyed.

New York Times, 1963

Everybody knows
New York
will never be completed.

Nynne Gottlieb, clothing designer

To **emphasize the prominence of** New York is like **pointing your finger at the moon.**

Andreas Bee, art historian

New York is like a big mess,
but once you step back,
it becomes a piece of art.

Thomas Zeumer, Metropolitan international

There is no question there is an unseen world; **the question is,** how far is it from midtown, and how late is it open?

Woody Allen, actor and director

Sometimes, from beyond the skyscrapers,
the cry of a tugboat finds you in your insomnia,
and you remember that
this desert of iron and cement is an island.

Albert Camus, French writer

New York is like a forest
of buildings.

Edgar Grospiron, French athlete

The city is not a concrete jungle,
it is a human zoo.

Desmond Morris, British anthropologist

It'll be a great place if they ever finish it.

O. Henry, American writer

I heard somebody say that New York is what Rome was two thousand years ago. **I like that.**

Christopher Walken, actor

New York is a great apartment hotel in which everyone lives and **no one is at home.**

Glenway Wescott, American writer

**No matter from which angle
New York hits your eyes –
they will ask for more.**

Edward C. Greenberg, attorney

Many cities remain **what they are,**
New York **constantly** reinvents itself.

Helmut Jahn, international architect

You know, the more they knock **New York,** the bigger it gets.

Will Rogers, American comedian

Traffic signals in New York are just rough guidelines.

David Letterman, Late Show Host

New York is the only real city–city.

Truman Capote, American writer

New York is so peaceful
from the fortieth floor.

Lorraine Bracco, actress

I tell you, there were times
when as Mayor,
I truly wanted to jump.

William O'Dwyer, former Mayor of the City of New York

I'd rather be a lampost **in New York than Mayor of Chicago.**

James J. Walker, former Mayor of the City of New York

The true New Yorker secretly believes
that people living anywhere else
have to be, in some sense, kidding.

John Updike, American writer

New York has a trip-hammer vitality
which **drives you insane**
with restlessness
if you have no inner stabilizer.

Henry Miller, American writer

I carry the place around
the world in my heart
but sometimes I try to
shake it off in my dreams.

F. Scott Fitzgerald, American writer

I've never walked in any other city
as much as I have in New York.
The eyes are filled with images
and my legs are constantly moving.

Jean–Christophe Ammann, former director
Museum für Moderne Kunst, Frankfurt/Main

Isn't it amusing how such an eruption of buildings adds up to such a pretty picture.

Spencer Drate, packaging designer

Once you reach Manhattan, you don't have **to cross any more bridges.**

Elisabeth Ernst, German artist

There's no room for amateurs, even in **crossing streets.**

George Segal, American artist

It's a town you come to for a short time.

Ernest Hemingway, American writer

The only city
where the sky is
not the limit.

Winka Dubbeldam, architect

When I think about **arriving in New York City, I anticipate** its vibrant and pulsating pace which creates **passionate feelings inside me.**

Elizabeth Taylor, actress

No place on earth unveils more contrast.

Herbert Pfeifer, industrial designer

When I think of New York,
I think of **surviving.**

Achim Degen, musician

The beautiful city,
the city of hurried
and sparkling waters!
the city of spires
and masts!
... my city!

Walt Whitman, American poet

**New York stretches the eyes
and invites me** to look at it
with renewed curiosity.

Caterine Milinaire, voyeuse

Everybody ought to have a
lower East Side **in their life.**

Irving Berlin, American songwriter

It used to be my playground
and it always will be.

Susanne Rüde, New York lover

New York's a place
where even the ugly
returns you to
the beautiful boundless soul
of its inhabitants.

Scott Elias, soul-based businessman

I mean that I was in love with the city, the way you love **the first person who ever touches you.**

Joan Didion, American writer

**The only credential the city asked
was the boldness to dream.**
For those who did, it unlocked its gates
and its treasures,
**not caring who they were
or where they came from.**

Moss Hart, American playwright

A hundred times have I thought
New York is a catastrophe,
and fifty times:
It is a beautiful catastrophe.

Le Corbusier, French architect

I've always thought that the look of New York, the architecture was fundamentally religious. Manhattan is a cathedral, you know – the modern cathedral.

Herbert Muschamp, architecture critic (New York Times)

New York is like **a series of** small towns.

Todd Webb, photographer

Skyscraper national **park.**

Kurt Vonnegut, American writer

Believe me, I know, when you leave New York, you go nowhere.

Laurence Fishburne, actor

1 Liberty Island
2 **South Cove, Battery Park City,** South Cove, Battery Park City
3 **Trinity Church / Wall Street,** Broadway/Wall Street
4 **Trinity Church,** Broadway/Wall Street
5 **New York Stock Exchange,** 8 Broad Street/Wall Street
6 **Park Avenue South,** Park Avenue South/34th Street
7 **Brooklyn Bridge,** Brooklyn, Water Street, Brooklyn
8 **Chrysler Building / Eagle,** 405 Lexington Avenue/42nd Street
9 **Bond Street, NoHo,** 20 Bond Street/Lafayette Street
10 **Avenue of the Americas,** 6th Avenue/50th Street
11 **Dia Center for the Arts,** 548 West 22nd Street/10th Avenue
12 **Twin Towers (destroyed in 2001) / Hotel Millenium,** Church/Vesey/West/Liberty Street
13 **49th Street, Rockefeller Center,** 6th Avenue/49th Street
14 **Empire State Building / 33rd Street,** 33rd Street/5th Avenue
15 **Trinity Church Graveyard,** Broadway/Wall Street
16 **Puck Building / Jersey Street,** 295–309 Lafayette Street/Mulberry Street
17 **Broadway, SoHo,** Broadway, Houston & Prince Street
18 **Bryant Park / New York Public Library,** 6th Avenue/41st Street
19 **Atlas, Rockefeller Center,** International Building, 5th Avenue/51st Street
20 **Cathedral St. John the Divine,** Amsterdam Avenue/112th Street
21 **Empire State Building / Park Avenue South,** 33rd Street/ Park Avenue South
22 **Gramercy & Flatiron District / North View,** 5th & 3rd Avenue/14th & 27th Street
23 **General Electric Building, Rockefeller Center,** Rockefeller Plaza
24 **Manhattan Bridge,** West Pillar
25 **American International Building, Financial District,** Pine/Pearl Street
26 **Central Park South,** 5th Avenue & Central Park West/59th & 110 Street
27 **Woolworth Building / Park Row,** 233 Broadway/Barclay Street
28 **Empire State Building / 7th Avenue,** 350 5th Avenue/34th Street
29 **Whitehall Building,** 17 Battery Place
30 **Steel Triangle, Rockefeller Center,** McGraw Hill Plaza, 6th Avenue/48th Street
31 **The Solomon R. Guggenheim Museum,** 1071 5th Avenue, 88th & 89th Street
32 **Municipal Building,** 1 Centre Street
33 **Moondance Diner, SoHo,** 6th Avenue/Grand Street
34 **Radio City Music Hall,** 6th Avenue/50th Street
35 **Woolworth Building / Warren Street,** 233 Broadway/Barclay Street
36 **Gramercy & Flatiron District / South View,** 5th & 3rd Avenue/14th & 27th Street
37 **Chrysler Building / Park Avenue South,** Park Avenue South/43rd Street
38 **Trump Tower,** 725 5th Avenue/54th Street
39 **Manhattan Bridge, Brooklyn,** Water Street/Washington Street, Brooklyn
40 **Water tower,** 12th Avenue/50th Street
41 **Empire State Building / Two Park Avenue South,** 350 5th Avenue/34th Street
42 **Broadway / Broome Street,** 487 Broadway/Broome Street
43 **Guggenheim Museum SoHo,** 575 Broadway/Prince Street
44 **AT&T Building / TriBeCa Tower,** 33 Thomas Street
45 **Grand Central Terminal,** Park Avenue South/42nd Street
46 **Brooklyn Bridge,** East Tower
47 **Nelson Tower,** 450 7th Avenue/34th Street
48 **Downtown Athletic Club / South Cove,** 21 West Street
49 **McGraw Hill Building, Rockefeller Center,** 6th Avenue/48th Street
50 **Saks Fifth Avenue,** 611 5th Avenue/50th Street
51 **Met Life Building,** 200 Park Avenue/45th Street
52 **Wall Street / New York Stock Exchange,** Wall Street
53 **World Trade Center (destroyed in 2001) / Little West Street,** Church/Vesey/West/Liberty St.
54 **Empire State Building / Broadway,** 350 5th Avenue/34th Street
55 **First Street, East Village,** 1st Street/1st Avenue
56 **Times Square,** Broadway/7th Avenue
57 **Flatiron Building,** 175 5th Avenue/Broadway & 23rd Street
58 **Citicorp Center,** 286 Lexington Avenue/53rd & 54th Street
59 **Houston Street,** Houston Street/Lafayette Street
60 **St. Patrick's Cathedral,** 5th Avenue/50th & 51st Street
61 **Clocktower,** 346 Broadway/Leonard Street
62 **Lipstick Building,** 885 3rd Avenue/53rd Street
63 **Broome Street, SoHo,** Broome Street/Crosby Street
64 **Sony Plaza,** 550 Madison Avenue/55th Street
65 **Central Park,** 5th Avenue & Central Park West/59th & 110th Street
66 **Statue of Liberty,** Liberty Island

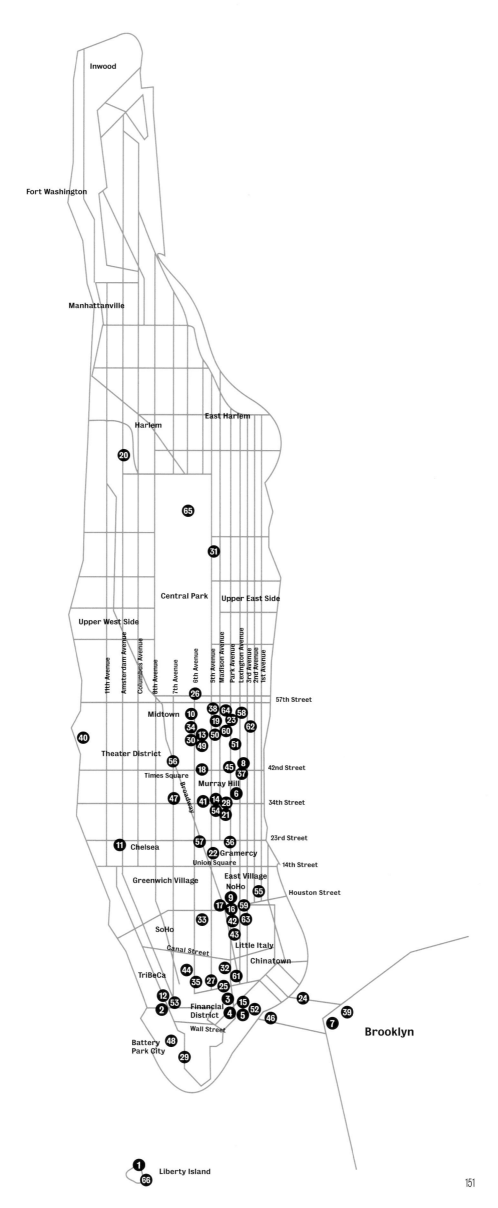

Inwood

Fort Washington

Manhattanville

East Harlem

Harlem

20

65

31

Central Park

Upper East Side

Upper West Side

57th Street

Midtown

26

11th Avenue
Amsterdam Avenue
Columbus Avenue
8th Avenue
7th Avenue
6th Avenue
5th Avenue
Madison Avenue
Park Avenue
Lexington Avenue
3rd Avenue
2nd Avenue
1st Avenue

10   38 64
        19 23   58
34
        50 60
13   62
30
49   51

40

Theater District

56

18   45   8
        37   42nd Street

Times Square

Murray Hill

6

Broadway

47   41 14 28
            54 21   34th Street

11   Chelsea

57   36   23rd Street

22   Gramercy

Union Square

14th Street

Greenwich Village

East Village
NoHo

55   Houston Street

9
17 16 59
33   42 63

SoHo

43

Little Italy

Canal Street

44   32   61   Chinatown

TriBeCa   35 27
                25

12 53   3   15
2   4   5   52
Financial
District   46   24   39

Wall Street   7   Brooklyn

Battery   48
Park City

29

1   Liberty Island

66

151

1 Liberty Island
A fascinating view of New York Bay and the unique skyline of Manhattan seen from Liberty Island.

2 South Cove, Battery Park City
The area around the World Trade Center (destroyed in 2001) has been the site of an urban development experiment for more than 20 years. The Hudson River Park above the South Cove seamlessly turns into Battery Park, the south tip of Manhattan. Like a phoenix from the ashes, Battery Park City and the World Financial Center rose at the beginning of the 1980s (Architects: Alexander Cooper and Stanton Eckstut). In 1967, 164 buildings were torn down for the construction of the World Trade Center alone. Millions of cubic feet of construction rubble and earth, dug up for the foundation of the Twin Towers, were dumped for the sake of convenience into the Hudson. Not long after, clever developers used the deposit for the grounds of Battery Park City, a "city within the city". City planning New York style.

3 Trinity Church / Wall Street
1839–1846
Architect: Richard Upjohn
In 1697 the Trinity Church parish had already been founded by means of a charter from King William III and at that time was ranked as one of the richest in the United States. The church building that had been erected in the 17th century fell victim to a fire in 1776; a succeeding building partially collapsed in 1830 and had to be torn down in 1839. The current Trinity Church with its 281-foot-high steeple was built from 1839 to 1846 in the Gothic Revival style according to the plans of architect Richard Upjohn. Until the turn of the century it was New York's highest monument and an important point of reference for navigation. Now Trinity Church, surrounded by gigantic skyscrapers, appears minute.

4 Trinity Church
See photo caption 3

5 New York Stock Exchange
Completed in 1903
Architect: G. B. Post
The largest stock market in the world hides behind the neoclassical facade with its ancient-world elements. It began very modestly: On May 17, 1792, with the signing of the Buttonwood Agreement, twenty-four brokers decided to regulate a chaotic financial market.

6 Park Avenue South
Within the street system of Manhattan, Park Avenue is unmistakable. At 42nd Street the Met Life Building separates the avenue into a south half and a north half.

7 Brooklyn Bridge, Brooklyn
1867–1883
Architect: John August Röbling
Led by the German-born American engineer John August Röbling, 600 people toiled almost sixteen years to complete the bridge. Twenty workers paid for this masterpiece with their lives and Röbling himself died as the result of a work-related accident. His son Washington, who from that point took over the project, also became seriously ill. It was his wife Emily who was able to complete the work of her father-in-law. In 1883 after the fourteen-mile-long steel cables had been strung between the granite neo-Gothic columns, the miraculous construction could display at last its purpose to 150,000 cheering New Yorkers.

8 Chrysler Building / Eagle
Completed in 1930
Architect: William van Alen
For a brief time this art deco building was the tallest skyscraper in the world. The architect William van Alen named the shiny chrome, 195-foot-high and 30-ton top Vertex. The stainless steel top was raised in just two hours with the help of a special crane and put into place at a height of 975 feet. The Chrysler Building topped the Eiffel Tower in Paris by sixty-eight feet.

9 Bond Street, NoHo
One of the most attractive buildings in NoHo (North of Houston Street) is all too often overlooked. But such "discoveries" make up the fascination of New York. Memories of "West Side Story" are awakened even though that site lies in the east, according to the city map.

10 Avenue of the Americas
No New Yorker would think of calling this avenue by its official name. In everyday use it is called simply "Sixth Avenue".

11 Dia Center for the Arts
One of the best known institutions for contemporary art is located near the Hudson River in Chelsea. The Dia Center was founded in 1974 by the former Munich gallery owner Heiner Friedrich with support from the Texas art collector Philippa de Menil. It became famous mainly through its two installations by the artist Walter de Maria: "The Broken Kilometer" in an exhibition space on West Broadway and "The New York Earth Room" in SoHo.

12 Twin Tower (destroyed in 2001) / Hotel Millenium
1970–1977
Architects: Minouri Yamasaki and Emery Roth & Sons
The 1375-foot high Twin Towers changed the profile of the southern tip of Manhattan in the middle of the 1970s forever. Till 2001 the Twin Towers have penetrated the sky over New York with their 110 stories. The owner, the Port Authority of New York and New Jersey, invested more than $ 600 million in the World Trade Center, which in addition to the Twin Towers includes five other buildings grouped around a plaza.

13 49th Street, Rockefeller Center
In 1928 John Davidson Rockefeller Jr. acquired tenancy rights from Columbia University and engaged an architectural committee under the direction of R. Hood Wallace and K. Harrison for a gigantic construction project. As a result of the stock market crash in 1929, construction work faltered.

14 Empire State Building / 33rd Street
1929–1931
Architects: Shreve, Lamb & Harmon
Simply immense, the top of the 1,248-foot-high skyscraper looms in the sky. Thus the Empire State Building asserts itself as the symbol of the most impressive skyline in the world. John Jacob Raskob, one of the financiers and vice president of General Motors, created a monument with this architectural milestone. At its dedication in 1931, the legendary classic had already broken all records: 102 stories, 1,860 steps, 6,500 windows and 73 elevators that could glide to the 85th floor within 90 seconds.

15 Trinity Church Graveyard
The date on the first gravestone in the oldest cemetery in New York is 1681. Among others, Robert Fulton, the inventor of the steamship, is buried here.

16 Puck Building/ Jersey Street
1885–1886; 1892–1893; 1899
Architects: A. Wagner, H. Wagner
The commercial building in neo-Romanesque style, which was erected in three construction phases at the end of the 19th century, served at first as the print shop and editorial offices of the satire magazine "Puck". The title refers to "Puck or Robin Goodfellow" in Shakespeare's "A Midsummer Night's Dream".

17 Broadway, SoHo
This traffic axis dates from the time of the Dutch settlers and was orginally called Breedweg. The present-day Broadway snakes its way from the south toward the north, the only diagonal street in Manhattan's right-angled street system. Broadway, with its 13 miles is not only the longest but also one of the oldest streets on the island.

18 Bryant Park/ New York Public Library
The small park next to the New York Library was laid out in 1871 and was named for the poet and journalist William Cullen Bryant. The site held a cemetery for the poor until 1823 and later a copy of the London Crystal Palace was built in 1853 on the occasion of the first American world exhibition. A fire in 1858 burned the supposedly fireproof glass building to the ground. The nearby public library has been in operation since 1911. The private book collections of the Astor, Lenox and Tilden families constituted the library's original stock. Today more than five million books are kept in the main building of the New York Public Library on Fifth Avenue.

19 Atlas, Rockefeller Center
1937
Sculptor: Lee Lawrie
Since 1937 the bronze Atlas with its globe has watched over St. Patrick's Cathedral on the opposite side of the avenue. The almost two-ton sculpture is one of twelve works by the sculptor Lee Lawrie that can be seen on the grounds of Rockefeller Center.

20 Cathedral St. John the Divine
Construction began in 1892
Architects: Heins & LaFarge, Cram & Ferguson
The cathedral rises majestically on the border to Harlem. The second-largest house of worship in the world looks back on a moving architectural story. When work on the church began in 1892 with the plans from Heins and LaFarge, the Episcopalian diocese was striving for a building with a neo-Romanesque look. After the death of the architects and Henry Codman Potter, the bishop responsible for the project, the style was radically changed in 1916. From then on the church was built in a neo-Gothic style designed by Ralph Adams Cram and Ferguson. To this day the scaffolding remains part of the look of the cathedral.

21 Empire State Building / Park Avenue South
See photo caption 14

22 Gramercy & Flatiron District / North View
Along with the Flatiron Building, the tower of the Metropolitan Life Insurance Company (1907–1909, architects: Napoleon LeBrun & Son) characterizes the look of Lower Fifth Avenue. The builders used the Campanile in the Piazza di San Marco in Venice as their architectural ideal. The original plans called for a building with 100 stories, but the worldwide economic crisis thwarted the insurance company's lofty plans.

23 General Electric Building, Rockefeller Center
1928–1973
Architects: R. Hood Wallace and K. Harrison
The RCA Building with its 70 stories and brilliant white limestone covering was christened in 1933. The entire complex consisting of nineteen multi-storied buildings was finally completed in 1973 with the last annex on the western side of Sixth Avenue. The statue of Prometheus, a gold-plated bronze created by Paul Manship, has graced the Lower Plaza since 1943. At Christmas time the largest evergreen in the world stands here.

24 Manhattan Bridge, West Pillar
Completed in 1909
Architects: Carrère & Hastings et al.
When the Manhattan Bridge was completed in 1909, it was supposed to relieve congestion on the Brooklyn Bridge, located just 270 yards away. In the meantime it has acquired a reputation as the most heavily-used bridge in New York with close to a half million commuters per year. Every day the subway rumbles by the almost endless line of cars on the bridge over the East River as it crosses the 485 yards that lie between Chinatown and Brooklyn.

25 American International Building, Financial District
After the opening of the New York Stock Exchange, all the internationally known banks moved into the Wall Street vicinity. In such close quarters, they had nowhere to go but "up". During the past 100 years the skyline east of Trinity Church has been changed completely by the innumerable skyscrapers.

26 Central Park South
Laid out in 1850
Architects: Frederick Law Olmsted and Calvert Vaux
Central Park was laid out in 1850 according to the plans of the landscape architects Frederick Law Olmsted and Calvert Vaux. The park, based on models of English landscapes, is the center of recreation in New York. It took sixteen years to create the rectangular 845-acre park. Its size surpasses the area of the Principality of Monaco.

27 Woolworth Building / Park Row
Completed in 1913
Architect: Cass Gilbert
The Woolworth Building was admired as the Eighth Wonder of the World. The neo-Gothic fairy tale castle, which also was described as "Mozart among the highrises", is one of the loveliest buildings that the New York skyline has to offer. From 1913 to 1930, the building had the honorary title of the highest building on Earth, but soon one New York height record after another was broken. Frank Woolworth, the proud owner, paid tribute to the miraculous building in his own style: he paid the $ 15 million invoice in cash.

28 Empire State Building / 7th Avenue
See photo caption 14

29 Whitehall Building
Although it has been overshadowed by showpiece projects like Battery Park City and the Twin Towers, the Whitehall Building, erected in the 1930s, has valiantly held onto its place on the southern tip of Manhattan.

30 Steel Triangle, Rockefeller Center
Design: Athelstan Spilhaus
The nearly sixty-five-foot-high steel sculpture, designed by Athelstan Spilhaus, enters into a dialogue with the surrounding high-rise buildings of Rockefeller Center. Reflections change the proportions according to the play of light.

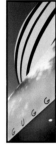

31 The Solomon R. Guggenheim Museum
1943–1959
Architect: Frank Lloyd Wright
Even Peggy Guggenheim insulted Frank Lloyd Wright's spectacular round building when she called it a "garage". The architect, who'd received his planning commission in 1943, fought for permission to build for almost fifteen years. He designed the exhibition hall as a 400-yard spiral-shaped ramp. Frank Lloyd Wright died in 1959, just six months before the opening of the museum. Now the "white stain" on the Upper East Side is famous for its unusual spiral form and is counted among the places of worship for art tourists from around the world.

32 Municipal Building
Completed in 1913
Architects: McKim, Mead & White
When the Bronx, Queens, Brooklyn and Staten Island became affiliated in 1898, the question was posed about an appropriate administrative site. With the completion in 1913 of the Municipal Building, built according to the plans of the architectural association of McKim, Mead and White, the representational need of Greater New York was satisfied. On the ground floor were neo-Baroque colonnades, over them a 14-story neo-Renaissance palace and as the crowning touch, obelisks, bell towers and a Civic Fame statue by Adolph A. Weinman. The Municipal Building is said to have impressed Stalin so much that he had Moscow's Lomonossow University built in a similiar style.

33 Moondance Diner, SoHo
SoHo is one of New York's trendiest neighborhoods. The locale of the Moondance Diner it is also the site of innumerable cafes, galleries and nightspots.

34 Radio City Music Hall
Completed in 1932
Architect: Donald Deskey
The largest concert hall in the world and one of the most popular attractions of Rockefeller Center was dedicated in 1932 and survives with its original furnishings intact. This typical American art deco temple has more than 6,200 comfortable seats, smoking salons and powder rooms.

35 Woolworth Building/ Warren Street
See photo caption 27

36 Gramercy & Flatiron District / South View
See photo caption 22

37 Chrysler Building / Park Avenue South
See photo caption 8

38 Trump Tower
Completed in 1983
Architects: Scutt of Swanke, Hayde, Connell & Partners
Named after its owner Donald J. Trump, the glass building built in 1983 tries with all its means to steal the show from its neighbors. Above all, the Atrium lures with its splendor and ostentation. Here the illuminated waterfall, walls of rose-colored marble and the shine of polished brass curry favor with the public. But the enterprising Trump has already moved onto other shores. On Columbus Circle his name soon will be engraved on a new building, housing what's proposed to be the tallest hotel in the city.

39 Manhattan Bridge
See photo caption 24

40 Water tower
Water towers are a part of the New York City image as much as yellow cabs and overflowing trash cans. Whether obviously visible or elegantly concealed, almost every building has a water tower on its roof. The container on the high-rises always assumes the task of regulating the water pressure. The model in use to this day was supposedly invented by a German immigrant and is derived, so it is said, from a sauerkraut barrel.

41 Empire State Building / Two Park Avenue South
See photo caption 14

42 Broadway / Broome Street
Built at the end of the 19th century
Architect: John T. Williams
This slender twelve-story terra-cotta-covered building stands out among the surrounding cast-iron architecture in SoHo. Erected at the end of the 19th century with the use of steel-frame technology, it was at that time the tallest building downtown.

43 Guggenheim Museum SoHo
1882; 1992
Architects: Thomas Stent; Arata Isozaki
The exhibition rooms in SoHo, designed as a subsidiary to the uptown Guggenheim Museum, were opened in 1992. The red brick building built in 1882 according to the plans of Thomas Stent was re-designed by Arata Isozaki with attention to the needs of the museum that has devoted itself to contemporary art.

44 AT&T Building / TriBeCa Tower
In this windowless colossus millions of switches are located in the building of the telephone company AT&T. Because they react very sensitively to light and temperature fluctuations, they are protected – as in Fort Knox – from the outside world with cement walls. However, the bunkerlike cement fortress disturbs the sensibility of the citys-cape in TriBeCa (Triangle Below Canal Street). The inhabitants of the area's tallest apartment building the TriBeCa Tower are not to be envied. Even though they moved into apart-ments above the clouds, they have to forego the view. The dreary cement wall of the AT&T Building looms directly in front of their windows.

45 Grand Central Terminal
Completed in 1913
Architects: Reed & Stern and Whitney Warren
The cornerstone for con-struction of the terminal was laid in 1872. Although the terminal was expanded in 1898 according to plans by William K. Vanderbilt, it was soon unable to hold its own against the increasing traffic volume. The large main concourse, designed by architects Reed & Stern and Whitney Warren, went into operation in 1913. Figures of Mercury, Hercules and Minerva grace the front of the beaux-arts temple. They symbolize the power of commerce, the strength of morality and the force of the intellect.

46 Brooklyn Bridge, East Tower
See photo caption 7

47 Nelson Tower
Completed in 1930
Architect: H. Craig Severance
The silhouette of Nelson Tower shows in exemplary fashion how the passing of the Zoning Resolution in 1916 affected the skyline of New York. So that enough light could fall into the street canyons, it was decreed that a building – depending upon the size of the lot and the width of the street – would have to taper off at the top.

48 Downtown Athletic Club / South Cove
1931
Architects: Starrett & van Vleck
The 535-foot-high building in the art deco style was completed in 1931. The early members of the elite Downtown Athletic Club came from the city's white anglo-saxon protestant population – as did Starrett and van Vleck themselves. Every year the club awards the coveted Heisman Trophy to the best college football player in the country.

49 McGraw Hill Building, Rockefeller Center
See photo caption 13

50 Saks Fifth Avenue
1924
Architects: Starrett & van Vleck
In 1902 Andrew Saks opened a department store on 34th Street. When his wealthy customers moved uptown, he decided to move with them. On the corner of 50th Street on Fifth Avenue, he built a palace in the neo-Renaissance style. Saks is famous for its window displays, which attract the curious especially in the weeks before Christmas.

51 Met Life Building
1958–1963
Architects: Walter Gropius, Emery Roth & Sons, TAC, Pietro Belluschi
The 800-foot office tower was erected over the tracks of Grand Central Station between 1958 to 1963 under contract to the airline company Pan Am. It was designed by an architectural group under the direction of Walter Gropius. In the beginning, the prismatic shape of the elegant skyscraper triggered a storm of protest because it brazenly blocked a main traffic artery. New Yorkers still refer to the 60-story building as "Pan Am" even though Met Life took over the building from the airline company in 1992.

52 Wall Street / New York Stock Exchange
Wall Street, the most famous address in the financial world today, formed the north border of the settlement called New Amsterdam. The name recalls a wall that was built as a defense to the city in the 17th century.

53 World Trade Center (destroyed in 2001) / Little West Street
See photo caption 12

54 Empire State Building / Broadway
See photo caption 14

55 First Street, East Village
The omnipresent fire escapes and graffiti are typical for this part of the city. The East Village constitutes a kind of self-contained village that enjoys increasing popularity. For this very reason it is feared that upscale redevelopment will change the character of the district.

56 Times Square
The center of the theater district, Times Square is dominated by neon advertising, billboards, and electronic banners. It is named for the "New York Times", which moved its editorial offices to the southern part of the square in 1916.

57 Flatiron Building
1902
Architect: D. H. Burnham
Due to its striking form, the tall, slim building whose layout is perfectly adapted to its wedge-shaped lot was given the nickname "Flatiron". Photographs by Alfred Stieglitz and Edward Steichen contributed to making the Flatiron Building, constructed at the beginning of the 20th century, the skyscraper par excellence.

58 Citicorp Center
1977
Architects: Hugh Stubbins & Associates
The 906-foot-high skyscraper with its shimmering aluminum skin rests on four gigantic stilts. The angled tower top not only gives the New York skyline an accent, but it also integrates solar collectors that deliver energy.

59 Houston Street
After the "Snowstorm of the Century" struck New York in March 1993, even a main traffic artery like Houston Street was turned into a magical and charming place of peace and quiet.

60 St. Patrick's Cathedral
1858
Architect: James Renwick
James Renwick presented New York with seven churches. St. Patrick's Cathedral, dedicated to Ireland's national saint, is undoubtedly one of his masterpieces. Built from 1858 to 1874, it is counted among the best Gothic Revival-style buildings that the United States has to offer.

61 Clocktower
The Clocktower crowns the New York Life Insurance Building and accommodates the galleries of the P.S.1 Institute of Contemporary Art.

62 Lipstick Building
1986
Architect: Philip Johnson
The oval windowfront resembles an enormous telescope focused on mid-town's sea of cement. The Lipstick Building was designed in the middle of the 1980s by Philip Johnson, now 90 years old, who is both a famous and controversial figure in the world of architecture. The onetime advocate of International Style became the pope of Post-Modernism in the 1980s. With his exhibition "Decon-structive Architecture", at the Museum of Modern Art in 1988, he once again coined a new term for a style of architecture.

63 Broome Street, SoHo
In SoHo (South of Houston Street) there are more commercial cast iron palaces than anywhere else in the world. Refined cast-iron technology made it possible in the middle of the 19th century to con-struct a building with ready-made elements that were fitted together on the site.

64 Sony Plaza
1984
Architects: Philip Johnson and John Burgee
The unique AT&T World Headquarters distinguishes itself with the unusual shape of its roof, to which it owes the name "Chippen-dale Skyscraper". Seen through the gap in the gable, clouds transform themselves into cotton candy. The high-rise in the rose-colored granite robe is a typical example of Post-Modern architecture.

65 Central Park
See photo caption 26

66 Statue of Liberty
Completed in 1886
Construction: Frédéric Auguste Bartholdi, Gustave Eiffel, Richard Morris Hunt
From far away the out-stretched torch of the Statue of Liberty, a symbol of freedom and indepen-dence, is visible to the new-comers of the New World. The statue, based on the design by Alsatian sculptor Frédéric Auguste Bartholdi, came to America as a gift from the French people. Gustave Eiffel saw to it that the robe of sheet copper was riveted to an ingenious steel girder construction. The resulting elasticity serves to help the statue withstand wind and weather.

New York, the vertical challenge

"A mind that is stretched to a new idea
never returns to its original dimension."
Oliver Wendell Holmes

This statement, sent to me by a good friend, has been hanging in my office for a few years. Now, as this book project about New York has come to an end, I see it as a sort of leitmotif for my work of the last five years.

Today I can't say exactly when the idea for New York Vertical came about. It developed slowly, at first on the fringes of my daily work. At some time between photography assignments and research in and about New York, it occurred to me that no one had yet looked at the city in a strictly vertical way. No publication about New York had devoted itself intensively to the very feature that is so characteristic of Manhattan.

Ten years ago I bought a used Linhof-Technorama. The unusual negative size of 2 ¼ by 6 ¾ got to me. Sensitized by my work with this camera, I came upon the black and white panoramas by the Prague photographer Josef Sudek (1896–1976). His work left a deep impact on me.

We naturally see things horizontally. The 98-degree sweeping perspective of the Technorama corresponds closely to the field of vision we can register with our eyes. I made my initial experiments with this photo axis. The accumulated knowledge formed the basis for New York's "vertical takeoff".

After the first vertical-view tests, I presented the results to the German publisher Bernhard Wipfler in October 1991. Enthusiastic about the photos, he decided to publish a book. Two years were estimated for the project. It turned out to be more. One year alone was necessary to get a grip on the extreme upright format. The technique determined the procedure. The 90mm fixed lens (Super Angulon) on the Technorama is comparable to a 24mm wide-angle lens on a 35mm camera. A spirit level is integrated in the detachable viewfinder to help the photographer balance out the hori-

zontal line. When the camera is turned vertically 90°, the optical middle axis in the viewfinder moves off-center. Due to this movement, the chosen shot has to be sought out and checked from top to bottom since it's impossible to see the whole picture at once. It was a long, drawn-out process until my eye was trained to make reliably good compositions. Especially when it involved capturing

parallel lines symmetrically, I had to take several exposures before I got what I wanted.

I had to figure out some focuses almost mathematically. For example, to capture the Nelson Tower's nearly fifty stories in this format without any distortion, I had to find a position between the 25th and 30th floors in the opposite building. That's when the problems began. Once in the building's elevator, it was like playing roulette: pick a number and hope it was the right one. On the chosen floor, I headed off in the right direction and approached the next hurdle: closed office doors behind which were usually surprised secretaries who had to be persuaded to let me go to the longed-for viewing spots. Most of the windows in New York can't be opened for safety reasons, so the last barrier, a reflecting pane of glass, had to be overcome with various tricks and gimmicks.

Each roll of film for this extreme size provided just four exposures. To keep out-takes to a minimum, I had to wait patiently for the right moment and, as far as possible, to avoid shaking and blurring. I couldn't count on a second chance. Besides that, it turned out that many ideal places were not accessible with a tripod.

The right lighting conditions determine a good picture. It is just this factor that is so difficult to predict. Permission to photograph at the wrong time didn't help much. I decided to use a highly sensitive film (Agfapan 400) so that I could – if necessary – take hand-held shots without giving up the shutter speeds. This proved to be the right decision. With only a camera and a few rolls of film in my pocket, I wasn't pegged as a photographer by stubborn doormen and curious elevator operators who let me into the buildings. Using this method, I was able to visit some locations up to 15 times until the light finally matched what I had in mind. The shock-absorbent central shutter in the lens made it easy to shoot with a hand-held camera. After thousands of photos, the Technorama and my shutter finger became good friends. In an emergency today, I can shoot at 1/15 of a second without losing the focus. Nevertheless, up to the last shot I had to improvise and to respond anew to every situation.

In the end it took four more years to treat the subject of New York Vertical. Copying such a project is something I recommend with some reservations because it demands, besides the

essential process of taking pictures, a string of other requirements: organisation and flexibility, absolutely no fear of heights, local knowledge and a memory for names, a fine-tuned sense of direction, lots of patience and doggedness, a pinch of brazenness, and above all, a good sense of humor. The act of photographing is reduced to a fraction of a second (shocking the thought that the sum of pure exposure time of the published photographs  doesn't even add up to two minutes). The trick lies in not losing your delight in the subject. Of course, this city won't allow itself to be captured completely, whether it's vertically, horizontally or diagonally. And that's exactly what makes it so fascinating. Every form of representation can be no more than another try. Looking at it that way

Stay vertical! Horst Hamann

biography

EXHIBITIONS (SELECTION)

1980	CARS AND STRIPES	Fotografische Sammlung Bongartz, Krefeld
1984	BILDER EINER AUSSTELLUNG	Künstlerhaus am Karlsplatz, Vienna
1985	KÜNSTLERPORTRAITS	Kunsthaus Hamburg, Hamburg
1986	KONFRONTATIONEN	Ernst Museum, Budapest
1991	BOTTICELLI MEETS BEUYS	Centre Culturel, Montpellier
1993	ABSOLUT MANHATTAN	Nikon House, New York
1994	IMAGES WITHOUT IMAGES	Electronic Nuyorican Poets Cafe, NY - LA - SF
1996	NEW YORK VERTICAL	Photokina, Cologne
1999	NEW YORK VERTICAL	Museum of the City of New York, New York
1999	NEW YORK VERTICAL	Internationale Fototage, Herten
1999	NEUE WEGE IN DER INDUSTRIEFOTOGRAFIE	Wilhelm-Hack-Museum, Ludwigshafen
2000	VERTICALS	Vanderbilt Hall, Grand Central Terminal, New York
2001	VERTICAL VIEW, 1991-2001	Center for Maine Contemporary Arts, Rockport, Maine
2001	CITY	Brooke Alexander Gallery, New York
2002	HORST HAMANN: NEW YORK	The Photographer's Gallery, London
2002	CONTRASTS	National Arts Club, New York
2002	NEW YORK	Michael Hoppen Gallery, London
2002	911	Library of Congress, Washington
2003	VERTICAL VIEW	Galerie Kasten, Art Chicago, Chicago
2003	DIE NEUE KUNSTHALLLE	Kunsthalle Mannheim, Mannheim
2004	NEW YORK VERTICAL	The Museum of Architecture, Photobiennale Moscow
2004	NEW YORK VERTICAL	Galerie IHN, Seoul
2005	PARIS VERTICAL	The French Cultural Center, Boston
2005	HORST HAMANN: NEW YORK 1:3	Kunsthalle Mannheim, Mannheim
2005	ONE NIGHT ON BROADWAY	Galerie Kasten, Mannheim
2005	PANORAMA DEUTSCHLAND	Museum für Kommunikation, Berlin

FILM (SELECTION)

1995	THEY DIDN'T KNOW...	Anti-AIDS short film, Madison Square Garden, New York
2001	910-911 NYC	Short film, 8 min., Script & Direction
2001	A SMILE GONE, BUT WHERE?	Short film after a story by Jimmy Breslin
2004	THE OTHER SIDE OF THE STREET	A documentary about Jimmy Breslin

BIBLIOGRAPHY (SELECTION)

1994	HUGHES, HOLLY STUART	'Horst Hamann loves New York' in PDN, New York 4/94
1996	HESS, HANS-EBERHARD	'New York Vertical' in PTI, Munich 9/96
1996	LANGER, FREDDY	So hoch - Horst Hamann fotografiert New York' in FAZ 227/96
1996	LANGEN, ANDREAS	'New York Vertikal' in Stuttgarter Zeitung 50/96
1997	WILLEMSEN, ROGER	'New York Vertical' in Vogue, München 1/97
1998	MACNEILLE, SUZANNE	'Head for Heights' in New York Times 3/98
1999	GUTTMANN, KATJA	'Horst Hamann/Portfolio' in Photographie 7-8/99 und 9/99
1999	ZOLLNER, MANFRED	'Horst Hamann - Paris Vertical' in Foto Magazin, Munich 11/99
1999	MUSCHAMP, HERBERT	'Steel Dreams That the Eye Can Cherish' in NYT 1/99
2001	SAEBISCH, BABETTE	'Der Waghalsige unter den Fotografen' in Der Frankfurter 3-4/01
2002	JONCKHEER, LIZ	'One Night on Broadway' in PDN, New York 11/02
2003	GRABER, BERND	'Trainspotting - Made In Germany' in Mannheimer Morgen 8/03
2003	MEERS, NICK	'Masters of Panorama Photography' in Stretch, RotoVision, UK
2004	PROFOTO RUSSIA	Moscow 14-4/2004
2004	GODRECHE, DOMINIQUE	5e Edition Photobiennale, Moscou, Photo France 409 05/04
2004	5TH INTERNATIONAL MONTH OF PHOTOGRAPHIE	Catalogue, Moscow, 2004
2005	INTERNATIONAL DAYS OF PHOTOGRAPHIE	Rhein-Neckar, 2005

BOOKS (SELECTION)

1992 ABSOLUT MANHATTAN N.Y. State of Mind Publishing, New York 1992
1996 NEW YORK VERTICAL Edition Panorama, Mannheim 1996
1999 FACES OF A COMPANY Edition Panorama, Mannheim 1999
2001 HORST HAMANN NEW YORK Edition Panorama, Mannheim 2001
2001 VERTICAL VIEW Edition Panorama, Mannheim 2001
2003 PANORAMA DEUTSCHE BAHN Edition Panorama, Mannheim 2003
2004 ONE NIGHT ON BROADWAY Schirmer/Mosel, Munich 2004
2004 PARIS VERTICAL Edition Panorama, Mannheim 2004
2005 VERTICAL NEW YORKERS Edition Panorama, Mannheim 2005
2006 DIE WELTMEISTER Edition Panorama, Mannheim 2006

TV & RADIO (SELECTION)

1995 SDR 3, SÜDDEUTSCHER RUNDFUNK TV (Klünder, Irene)
'Portrait; Horst Hamann über New York' in Landesschau, Stuttgart
1997 ARD, SÜDDEUTSCHER RUNDFUNK TV (Krupok, Isolde)
'Horst Hamann in New York' in Mensch, Leute!, Stuttgart
1997 ARTE - TV (Pütz, Günter)
'Horst Hamann und seine vertikale Sichtweise' in Metropolis, Strasbourg
1998 ZDF ZWEITES DEUTSCHES FERNSEHEN TV (Hess, Jutta)
'New York im Hochformat - die Fotos von Horst Hamann' in Aspekte, Mainz
1998 SWF, SÜDWESTFUNK TV (Buettner, Tilmann)
'Im Schatten der Wall Street' in USA , Baden-Baden
1998 WNBC - TV (Taylor, Felicia)
'Horst Hamann at the Museum of the City of New York' in Sunday Today, New York
1999 SWR, SÜDWESTRUNDFUNK TV (Kilwink, Isa)
'Der Senkrechtstarter' in Nahaufnahme, SWR, Mainz
1999 BBC - TV (Potter, Elisabeth)
'New York Vertical at the Museum of the City of New York' in BBC News, New York
1999 PBS - TV (Deroy, Jaimee)
'Vertical Photographs at the Museum of the City of New York' in City Arts, New York
1999 ARTE - TV (Burchardt, Melanie)
'Big Apple bei den Fototagen' in Herten, in Tracks Straßburg
1999 SWR 3, SÜDWESTRUNDFUNK RADIO (Ries, Michael)
'Studiogast Horst Hamann' in Leute, Stuttgart
1999 SWR, SÜDWESTRUNDFUNK TV (Hattensen, Maja)
'Neue Wege in der Industriefotografie' in Kulturreport, Mainz
1999 HR 3, HESSISCHER RUNDFUNK TV (Soliman, Tina)
'Mr. Vertical' in Moderne Menschen, Frankfurt
2002 BBC SCOTLAND (Morton, Brian)
'Live Gäste incl. Norman Mailer, Horst Hamann' in BBC, Edinburgh/New York
2003 SWR, SÜDWESTRUNDFUNK TV
'Studiogast Horst Hamann' in Kultur Cafe, Baden-Baden

COLLECTIONS (SELECTION)

AGFA GEVAERT COLLECTION, Leverkusen
FOTOGRAFISCHE SAMMLUNG BONGARTZ, Krefeld
MUSEUM OF THE CITY OF NEW YORK, New York
SAATCHI COLLECTION, London
PORTLAND MUSEUM OF ART, Portland
GOLDMAN SACHS COLLECTION, New York
MOSCOW HOUSE OF PHOTOGRAPHIE, Moscow

thank you

For their loyalty and support, I thank:
Maria Hamann, Heinrich Gröger, Johannes Hamann, Andreas Bee

For his courage and trust, I thank:
the publisher Bernhard Wipfler

Grateful acknowledgement for permission to use quotations to:
William Rossa Cole, New York
Bill Henderson; Pushcart Press, Long Island
Interview Magazine, New York; Ingrid Sischy, Barbara Carlyle, Gisela Williams, Stephanie Rosenfeld

Heartfelt thanks to:
Jack Deacy

For their generous support, I thank the following companies and individuals:
Agfa Leverkusen, especially Hansjoachim Nierentz
Agfa Division, New Jersey, Peter Lebovitz
68 Degrees, New York; Patricia Katchur, Chris Meyer, Fred Castillo
Modernage, New York; Kenneth Troiano and George Coste
Foto Schwetasch (Marcus, Gerd, Linde, Sibylle), Seckenheim

My special thanks go to:
David Rowland, J. J. Straub, Wolfgang Roth, Andrea Hambuechen, Barbette Havriliak, Tilo Kaiser, Thomas Zeumer, Serafine Klarwein, Marcus Nispel, Werner Bochmann, Roberto Costa, Sabine E. Rieck, Susan Nicholas (International Center of Photography), Astrid Hamann, Andrea Dörr, Kate Simmons, Eric Schloss, Judith Stonehill (New York Bound Bookshop), Orysia Germak (New York Island Helicopters), Robert Häusser, Marli Hoppe-Ritter, Volker Skierka, Herbert Pfeifer, Renate Claus (Dia Print Richter, Heidelberg), Carl Weissner, Edward C. Greenberg, Matthias Held, Taki Wise (Staley & Wise Gallery), Hans-Eberhard Hess, Maria Pignataro, Chen Sam, Mimi Brown, Screen Actors Guild New York, Heinz-Dietrich Olberg, Cornelia Franz, Annette Tietenberg, Kevin Breslin, Hendrik te Neues, Cécile zu Hohenlohe, Stephen Hulburt, Calvin Ki, Lloyd Peterson

My thanks also apply to:
Hisao Oka, Masashi Ohtsu, Elisabeth Ernst, Susanne Rüde, Hans and Annemarie Wohlfarth, Meike Wohlfarth, Dominique, Christiane, Claire, Laurent Préaud, Babette Grospiron, Stephanie Préaud, Philip Tsiaras, Monroe, Janneke de Vries, Sonja Bullaty, Angelo Lomeo, Dennis & Diane Griggs, Nelly Siet, Harald Pfannebecker, Ilona Ortner, Friedemann Leinert, Rita Rivera, Jessica Miller, Len Stein, J. Travis (Visibility), Leah Levin, Nathan Hill, Michael Grohmann, Annette Skierka, Daniela Denninger, Dieter Fuchs, Katarina Driesch, Joram Harel, Martin Stather, Manfred Metzner, Irene Klünder, Stephan Wolf, Lorin W. Finkelstein, Hannah Wittich, Tim, Kenneth Sussmane, Philip Meunier, Elena Muldoon, Matthias Hamann, Stefanie Hamann, Lutz Bernstein, Detlev Meinerz, Doug Bagelman, Werner Schwarzer, Rosi Thielen, Tina and Dieter Tassis-Iffland, Isabel Tassis, Uwe Block, Wolfgang Rolli, Irmgard Kuhn-Geiselhart, Martine Barrat, Sven Mader, Freddy Cushing, Ruby Babooran, Todd's Copy, Maria Jung, Victoria Eichinger & Peter Baumann, Thomas and Susan Plagemann, Klaus Kleinschmidt, Peter Scholler, Imke Culmann, Martina Eifler, Frank Aschermann, Kristian and Susanne Rahtjen, Ike Jörn, Marcus Tiedemann, Michal Hirsch, Achim Degen, Vincent Oster, Peter Rösel, Donna, Arie Kopelman, Holger Laufenberg, Klaus Meine, Rudolph Schenker, Nora Küppers, Jochen Sendler and Bertin, Adam Osterfeld, Jannice Hogan, Xandi Borchers, Matthias Schmid, Wolfgang Pachali, Daniela Thurn, Martin Gottschall, Hans-Peter Suchan, Werner Riehm, Jürgen Briller, Egon Zippel, Nathan Hill, Fritz E. Richter, Klaus von Taschitzki, Matthias Biebel, Ismail Dogan, Rüdiger Lutz, Leo Strohm, John Bruno, Chrysler Corporation, (Cushman & Wakefield), Bernd Rupp, Thomas König, Karin König, Anja Bochmann, Klaus Hecke, Udo Klein, Suzanne Jacoby, Ulrike Ningel, Ndidi Nnoli, Anja & Wolfgang Roth, Emulsion New York, Claudia Strand, Mr. & Mrs. Gellner, Franz Fetzer, Margueritte Barra, Rainer Kubelka, Alex Müller, Gretel & Roman Eisinger Niedworok, Sabine Schmitt, Sebastian Wipfler, Reinhold Jeutner, Susan Klein

For their personal contributions, I thank:
the former Mayor of the City of New York Rudolph W. Giuliani, J. J. Straub, Noritoshi Hirakawa, Serafine Klarwein, Marcus Nispel, William Rossa Cole, Nynne Gottlieb, Andreas Bee, Thomas Zeumer, Edgar Grospiron, Edward C. Greenberg, Helmut Jahn, Kevin Breslin, Jean-Christophe Ammann, Spencer Drate, Elisabeth Ernst, Winka Dubbeldam, Elizabeth Taylor, Herbert Pfeifer, Achim Degen, Caterine Milinaire, Susanne Rüde, Scott Elias, Todd Webb, Wolfgang Joop, Laurence Fishburne

And all New Yorkers

And not least of all, I thank Jeanne-Claude and Christo, for their friendly advice to have the distorting vertical lines cleaned from my overworked fax machine.

imprint

Published internationally by teNeues Publishing Group:
Kempen, Düsseldorf, London, Madrid, New York, Paris
© 1996 EDITION PANORAMA and Horst Hamann
© Verticals photography: Horst Hamann
© photography back cover and page 159, 161:
Marie Hamann
© photography page 160: Lorin Finkelstein

Editor: Bernhard Wipfler
Editorial department New York: Marie Hamann
Editorial department Germany: Annette Tietenberg,
Cornelia Franz
Translation: Kate Simmons
Design: Harold Vits & bureau für gestaltung
Cover design: Calvin Ki, Harold Vits
Map: Roberto Costa
Separations: Werner Bochmann, Scantronic
Printing: abcdruck GmbH, Heidelberg
Binding: Schaumann, Darmstadt
© Quotations reproductions: 1, 2, 9, 14, 16, 17, 20, 21, 22,
25, 30, 31, 41, 43, 45, 46, 49, 50, 51, 52, 54, 57, 58, 63, 64, 66
Horst Hamann and authors
© Quotations reproductions: 28, 35, 62 courtesy of
Interview Magazine, New York.
© All other reproductions: courtesy of William Rossa
Cole 1992 from Quotable New York – A Literary
Companion, Bill Henderson, Pushcart Press. With kind
permission.

www.editionpanorama.de

A Production by EDITIONPANORAMA Germany
Publisher Bernhard Wipfler

www.horsthamann.com

www.editionpanorama.de

www.teneues.com